Montana

Jim Ollhoff

Visit us at
www.abdopublishing.com

Published by ABDO Publishing Company, 8000 West 78th Street, Suite 310, Edina, Minnesota 55439 USA. Copyright ©2010 by Abdo Consulting Group, Inc. International copyrights reserved in all countries. No part of this book may be reproduced in any form without written permission from the publisher. The Checkerboard Library™ is a trademark and logo of ABDO Publishing Company.

Printed in the United States.

Editor: John Hamilton
Graphic Design: Sue Hamilton
Cover Illustration: Neil Klinepier
Cover Photo: iStock
Interior Photo Credits: Alamy, Airphoto-Jim Wark, AP Images, Charles M. Russell, Clymer Museum of Art/John F. Clymer, Comstock, Corbis, Custer Battlefield Museum, David Olson, Dennis Dickerson, Getty, Granger Collection, Independence National Historical Park/C.W. Peale, iStock Photo, Jerry Ting, Katie LaSalle-Lowery, Library of Congress, Mile High Maps, Montana Historical Society/Edward S. Paxson, Montana State University, Mountain High Maps, One Mile Up, State of Montana, USPS, and University of Montana.
Statistics: State population statistics taken from 2008 U.S. Census Bureau estimates. City and town population statistics taken from July 1, 2007, U.S. Census Bureau estimates. Land and water area statistics taken from 2000 Census, U.S. Census Bureau.

Manufactured with paper containing at least 10% post-consumer waste

Library of Congress Cataloging-in-Publication Data

Ollhoff, Jim, 1959-
  Montana / Jim Ollhoff.
     p. cm. -- (The United States)
  Includes index.
  ISBN 978-1-60453-661-4
  1. Montana--Juvenile literature. I. Title.

F731.3.O45 2010
978.6--dc22
                        2008051717

Table of Contents

Big Sky Country

Montana is sometimes called "Big Sky Country." Its mountains, scenic forests, and wide-open plains make the sky look like it goes on forever. It's one of the biggest states, but one of the states with the fewest people.

Montana is rich in history. The state is the home of many Native American tribes, including the Cheyenne and Blackfoot. Lewis and Clark traveled through Montana in 1805 and 1806. Gold rushes, copper mines, and huge ranches made Montana a Wild West state.

Today, Montana has some of the most magnificent scenery in the world. Glacier National Park, mountain ranges, wildlife refuges, and endless horizons show off Montana's natural beauty.

A mountain goat in Montana's Glacier National Park.

Quick Facts

MONTANA

Name: From a Spanish word meaning "mountainous."

State Capital: Helena, population 28,726

Date of Statehood: November 8, 1889 (41st state)

Population: 967,440 (44th-most populous state)

Area (Total Land and Water): 147,042 square miles (380,837 sq km), 4th-largest state

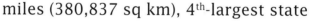

Largest City: Billings, population 101,876

Nicknames: Big Sky Country; Treasure State; Mountain State; Bonanza State

Motto: *Oro y plata* (Gold and Silver)

State Bird: Western Meadowlark

Sapphire & Agate

Granite
Peak

Kootenai River

State Flower: Bitterroot

State Gemstone: Sapphire and Agate

State Tree: Ponderosa Pine

State Song: "Montana"

Highest Point: Granite Peak, 12,799 ft (3,901 m)

Lowest Point: Kootenai River, 1,800 ft (549 m)

Average July Temperature: 68°F (20°C)

Record High Temperature: 117°F (47°C) at Glendive on July 20, 1893

Average January Temperature: 27°F (-3°C)

Record Low Temperature: -70°F (-57°C) at Rogers Pass, on January 20, 1954

Average Annual Precipitation: 13 inches (33 cm)

Number of U.S. Senators: 2

Number of U.S. Representatives: 1

U.S. Postal Service Abbreviation: MT

Geography

Montana is bordered by Canada to the north. Wyoming is to the south and Idaho to the west. To the east are North and South Dakota.

The Missouri River begins in the mountains of western Montana. It flows eastward across the state, into North Dakota. The Missouri River wanders its way down to the state of Missouri. Lewis and Clark followed the Missouri River on their journeys from 1804 to 1806. The other major rivers in Montana include the Clark Fork River and the Yellowstone River.

The Continental Divide is in Montana, right along the Rocky Mountains.

Path of the Continental Divide

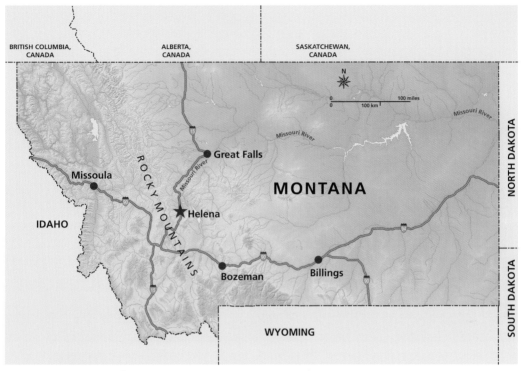

Montana's total land and water area is 147,042 square miles (380,837 sq km). It is the 4th-largest state. The state capital is Helena.

An aerial view of Montana's Rocky Mountains.

The western part of Montana is filled with many mountains. There are more than 50 mountain ranges on the western side of the state. They are part of the Rocky Mountains. The Rockies start in Canada, cut across western Montana, and go into Wyoming and Colorado.

The eastern side of the state is made up of gently rolling hills. It is part of the Great Plains, an area of relatively flat land in the central United States.

In the south central section of the state is part of Yellowstone National Park. Most of Yellowstone is in Wyoming. This park has the world's most active geysers. A geyser is a spring that spews up hot water with explosive force from time to time.

In the northwestern corner of the state is Glacier National Park, where majestic mountains were cut by huge glaciers long ago.

A double rainbow forms over the mountains in Glacier National Park.

Climate and Weather

Montana is famous for its bitterly cold winters. In fact, the coldest temperature ever recorded in one of the 48 contiguous states was in Montana. It

A heavy Montana snowstorm.

reached minus 70 degrees Fahrenheit (-57°C). However, winter cold spells are often short. Warm winds from the west, called chinook winds, help ease the cold.

Montana is a large state with different kinds of geography. This causes different kinds of weather. On the western side of Montana, the mountains determine climate. The higher elevation creates colder temperatures. It is also snowier in the higher elevations.

Certain areas of Montana get little rainfall, creating a dry landscape.

There isn't a lot rainfall in the eastern part of the state. The western mountains block the moist air coming from the Pacific Ocean.

Plants and Animals

The western side of Montana is woods. About 25 percent of the state is covered in forests. Common types of forest trees include Douglas fir, ponderosa pine, lodgepole pine, and Rocky Mountain maple.

On the mountains, there is an elevation called the "tree line." Above the tree line, trees do not grow. It may be too cold for trees, or snow may cover the area all year long. The elevation of the tree line depends on the mountain range. For the Rocky Mountains, the tree line is often between 10,000 and 12,000 feet (3,048-3,658 m).

Above the tree line, there is light tundra vegetation. Rocks, snow, and glaciers cover most of this cold land.

Much of Montana is covered in forests. However, on the mountains, above the tree line, trees do not grow.

Big animals like to live in the mountains. Grizzly bears, Rocky Mountain goats, bighorn sheep, and moose make their home in the mountains. Elk, black bears, mountain lions, lynx, and bobcats also enjoy the forest cover of the mountains.

On the eastern side of the state, the land is mostly short grassland called the plains. Coyotes, badgers, mule deer, and pronghorns live in this area.

All over the state are beavers, deer, muskrats, and mink. Bald eagles, ducks, and geese can also be found throughout Montana. In spring, when snow geese migrate, they travel through Montana's Freezeout Lake area. During this time, it is possible to see 300,000 snow geese and 10,000 tundra swans.

Many flowers are native to Montana. These include primroses, lilies, orchids, daisies, and bitterroots (the state flower).

Lynx cub and daisies

Bighorn sheep grazing.

Grizzly Bear

Moose Calf

Snow Geese

History

People have lived in Montana for at least 9,000 years, and probably much earlier. By the 1800s, Native American

Two Crow Indians on horseback in Montana, photographed in 1905.

tribes lived all over the state. The Crow Indians lived in the south, the Cheyenne lived in the southeast. The Assiniboine and Atsina lived in the north. The Kootenai and Salish lived in the west. The Blackfoot lived in the central part of the state.

The first known white explorers in Montana were Lewis and Clark. They traveled through the area in 1805 and 1806. Their expedition followed the Missouri River westward, and then crossed the Rocky Mountains.

The Lewis and Clark Expedition explored parts of Montana.

Soon after Lewis and Clark, fur traders and trappers began to move in and out of the state. They set up forts to trade with the Native Americans. The only surviving fort from that time is Fort Benton. It was officially established as a town much later.

Roman Catholic missionaries came to Montana after the trappers. They built a mission near Stevensville in 1841. It is considered the first permanent settlement in Montana.

Towns were created and shut down overnight when treasure-hunters arrived and then left.

In the 1860s, gold was discovered. This brought gold-hunters and treasure-seekers. Towns arose overnight. But, when the gold ran out, many towns were quickly abandoned.

In 1864, the United States federal government created Montana Territory. This brought settlers into the area.

As more and more settlers came to Montana, the Native Americans began to lose their homeland and hunting grounds. They fought back. The Lakota Sioux and Cheyenne won the Battle of the Little Bighorn in 1876 against U.S. Army forces led by Lieutenant Colonel George Custer. However, it would be the last major battle the Native Americans would win.

Cattle ranches began to spread in the 1870s. The mining towns wanted beef, so ranching became important. Railroads were built across Montana in the 1880s.

In 1889, Montana became a state. Silver and copper were discovered near Butte, which brought even more people to the state. Oil and natural gas were discovered in the early 1900s.

The Battle of the Little Bighorn.

After World War I, many of Montana's wheat farmers could no longer afford to farm. A long drought had hurt the crops, and a price drop in wheat made it difficult to make a living. In 1929, the Great Depression brought financial problems to the people of Montana. A number of government projects in the 1930s eventually helped the state out of its depression.

In this photo, taken in the 1930s, men work for the government breaking rocks to build a truck trail in Deerlodge National Forest, Montana.

After the end of World War II in 1945, a slow shift occurred from mining toward other industries. While mining was still important, tourism became the second-largest industry. Agriculture was still the state's largest industry. By the 1980s, most of the copper mines were closed.

An ore shovel waits to load a truck at an open pit copper mine in Butte, Montana. Many people lost their jobs when the copper mines closed.

Did You Know?

Lt. Colonel George Custer.

The Battle of the Little Bighorn is sometimes called Custer's Last Stand. Lakota Sioux and Northern Cheyenne Native Americans won this battle against Lieutenant Colonel George Custer and the U.S. Army's 7th Cavalry on June 25, 1876. The way the United States government dealt with the Native Americans was often unfair and brutal. In 1868, the government said that the native tribes could have the land west of the Missouri River.

Crazy Horse and Sitting Bull were Native American leaders.

However, gold was discovered in that area. Even though some of those lands were sacred to the Indians, white gold hunters rushed in. The U.S. government didn't stop the miners. In fact, the Native Americans were told to leave their lands and settle on the reservations. The natives did not want to leave, and fought to stay.

By 1876, the government sent Army troops to find the Indians and force them onto reservations. Lieutenant Colonel George Custer rushed his cavalry into battle before more Army troops could arrive. Custer met a combined force of Lakota Sioux and Cheyenne at the Little Bighorn River. The Indian warriors soundly defeated Custer, leaving him and more than 200 of his troops dead.

A scene from the Battle of the Little Bighorn.

People

Paleontologist Jack Horner with the fossilized egg nest of a duck-billed dinosaur.

Jack Horner (1946-) is a paleontologist, a person who studies dinosaur fossils. He was born and raised in Shelby, Montana. He is one of the most well-known fossil hunters in the United States. He has made many important discoveries. He was the scientific advisor on the movie *Jurassic Park*. Despite a learning disability, he is a well-respected professor at Montana State University Bozeman.

Congresswoman
Jeannette Rankin
(1880-1973) was born
and raised on a ranch
in Missoula, Montana.
Rankin graduated from
the University of Montana
in 1902. In 1916, she
became the first woman
to be elected to the
United States House of
Representatives.

Rankin worked
tirelessly for peace and for the rights of women.
She campaigned against forcing children to work in
factories. She was the only legislator to vote against
the United States' entry into World War II.

Artist **Charles Marion Russell** (1864-1926) was born in Missouri, but was always fascinated with the Old West. When he was 16 years old, he moved to a ranch in the Judith Basin of Montana. His father thought Charles would only be there for the summer, but the teen loved the state. He stayed in Montana for the rest of his life. He specialized in painting scenes of the Old West, such as cowboys, Native Americans, and landscapes. The C.M. Russell Museum is in Great Falls, Montana, the town where he lived.

A 1902 painting by Charles M. Russell.

Gary Cooper (1901-1961) was born near Helena, Montana. He began acting in Hollywood films in 1925, and made more than 100 movies in his career. He often played characters that were tough but quiet heroes, who set out to do the right thing. During his career, he won two Academy Awards, the highest honor in Hollywood. In 1999, the American Film Institute named him to the list of greatest male actors of all time.

Cities

Billings began in 1877 as a steamboat stop along the Yellowstone River. In 1882, railroads were

built through Montana, and Billings was an important stop along the tracks. Billings has enjoyed constant growth over the years. It is the largest city in Montana, with a population of 101,876. There are several colleges in the city, including Montana State University Billings.

Bozeman is the fifth-largest city in Montana, with a population of 37,981. It was named after explorer John Bozeman.

Today, downtown Bozeman has many historic buildings. The Museum of the Rockies is part of Montana State University Bozeman. Visitors can see the largest *Tyrannosaurus rex* skull ever found.

Cathedral of St. Helena

Helena is the capital of Montana. Its population is 28,726. It was founded in 1864, after the discovery of gold in Last Chance Creek. There are many historic buildings in the city, including the Civic Center and the Cathedral of St. Helena.

Great Falls is named after a series of waterfalls in the area. Lewis and Clark, in their journey of 1804-1806, had to walk around these falls. The city of Great Falls was planned and founded by businessmen Paris Gibson and James J. Hill in 1884. They believed that the area's businesses

could use the waterpower from a dam on the Missouri River. Great Falls quickly became an industrial center. Several military facilities have been built in and around Great Falls. With a population of 58,827, it is the third-largest city in Montana.

Missoula is the second-largest city in Montana, with a population of 67,165. In 1805, Lewis and Clark came through the Missoula Valley. The U.S. Army created Fort Missoula in 1877. Railroads came through in 1883, creating a trading center. The main campus

Smokejumper training.

of the University of Montana is in Missoula. The U.S. Forest Service's Missoula Smokejumper Base is near the Missoula International Airport. Firefighters take on the dangerous job of controlling and putting out remote wilderness fires.

Transportation

The main interstate highways in Montana are I-15, I-94, and I-90. Interstate I-15 goes north and south, from the Canadian province of Alberta, through Montana, and then towards Idaho Falls, Idaho. Interstate I-90 goes east and west. From the Idaho border, it stretches across the state and then exits south into Wyoming. Interstate I-94 enters Montana at the North Dakota border, then links with I-90 at Billings.

Bear Country

All Wildlife Is Dangerous
Do Not Approach Or Feed

Wildlife warnings are often seen on Montana roadways.

Amtrak carries visitors to Montana's Glacier National Park.

There are seven main airports in Montana. Four of them are international airports, which means travelers can come and go from other countries. The largest airport is in Billings. There are more than 100 smaller airports, airfields, and heliports in Montana.

Amtrak provides train service through Montana. Bus companies also provide routes between cities.

Natural Resources

Mining has always been important to Montana. Gold, silver, copper, platinum, and other minerals are plentiful on the western side of the state. Oil was discovered in 1915. Coal, oil, and natural gas continue to be mined.

A gold miner drills for ore at a mine in Gardiner, Montana.

The forests on the western side of the state provide lumber. Pine, western larch, fir, and spruce trees are spread out over millions of acres. Plywood, paper, and other paper products are manufactured from the lumber.

The north central and eastern parts of Montana have large areas of soil that are perfect for growing wheat. Much of this land is also used to grow grass for sheep and cattle.

Water provides hydroelectric power for much of the state. Several large dams, such as the Fort Peck Dam on the Missouri River, provide hydroelectric power and water to help to irrigate farmlands.

Completed in 1940, Fort Peck Dam on the Missouri River provides water and hydroelectric power to the area.

Industry

Agriculture brings in a lot of money to Montana. Beef cattle and sheep are raised on ranches all over the state. Farmers grow grains, sugar beets, potatoes, and fruit. Wheat is Montana's leading cash crop. The best wheat-growing areas are in the north central part of the state.

Cowboys round up mustangs.

Many Montana residents live in rural areas.

Sometimes, Montana is called "the most rural state." More than one-third of Montana's residents live in a rural county, more than any other state.

Mining has been historically important, but less so today. Most of the copper mines closed in the 1980s.

Tourism has grown in importance. Each year, millions of people visit Glacier and Yellowstone National Parks, as well as the site of the Battle of the Little Bighorn. Montana is home to many places of natural beauty and historic interest.

A wrangler takes horses to tourists for an early morning ride in Glacier National Park.

Sports

The Grizzlies and Bobcats are popular Montana college teams.

There are no major league sports teams in Montana. However, a number of cities have minor league teams, including Billings, Butte, and Missoula. College sports teams are popular, including the University of Montana Grizzlies and the Montana State University Bobcats.

Montana's many mountains make it a great place for skiing and snowboarding. Sled dog races and snowmobiling are also popular.

With such vast areas of land, opportunities for hiking and backpacking are endless. It is sometimes easy for hikers to get lost in the remote mountains. It is important for hikers to have backcountry survival skills.

Fishing and hunting are popular pastimes. Most lakes and large rivers can be fished throughout the year. Watching birds and other wildlife can be exciting anywhere in Montana, but it is very popular in the national parks and wildlife refuges.

A kayaker goes over Kootenai Falls on Montana's Kootenai River.

Entertainment

The Montana Arts Council is a state agency. It funds local organizations that create music, drama, dance,

literature, and visual arts. The Montana Institute of Arts, founded in 1948, has publications and exhibits for Montana artists. They hold an annual art festival.

Native American tribes hold traditional dance ceremonies and powwows. Rodeos can be found all over the state.

A boy dances during a Native American festival.

Many museums in the state are dedicated to dinosaurs. Some museums feature actual dinosaur digs.

Billings is the home of ZooMontana. This huge zoo specializes in animals found in the northern states. The exhibits are constructed to look like the animals' natural habitats. More than 70,000 people visit every year.

The world's largest *Tyrannosaurus rex* skull is on display at the Museum of the Rockies in Bozeman, Montana.

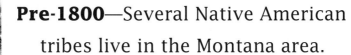

Timeline

Pre-1800—Several Native American tribes live in the Montana area.

1803—The United States buys much of present-day Montana from France in the Louisiana Purchase.

1805-1806—Lewis and Clark explore the Montana area.

1847—Fort Benton is founded as a trading and military post.

1864—The federal government organizes Montana Territory.

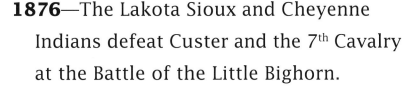

1876—The Lakota Sioux and Cheyenne Indians defeat Custer and the 7th Cavalry at the Battle of the Little Bighorn.

1880s—Railroads are built across the state.

1889—Montana becomes the 41st state in the Union.

1890-1891—The first dam and hydroelectric facility is built on the Missouri River's Black Eagle Falls.

1940—Fort Peck Dam is completed.

2000—Summer fires burn nearly 1,000,000 acres (404,686 ha) and destroy 320 homes in the Bitterroot Valley.

Glossary

Battle of the Little Bighorn—A battle in 1876 between the U.S. Army, led by Lieutenant Colonel George Custer, and the Lakota Sioux and Cheyenne tribes.

Contiguous—Connected or touching. For example, 48 of the 50 United States are contiguous. Alaska and Hawaii do not share borders with any of the other states.

Continental Divide—A ridge of the Rocky Mountains in North America. Water flowing west of the divide goes to the Pacific Ocean. Water flowing east eventually goes to the Atlantic Ocean.

Glacier—A huge, slow-moving sheet of ice that grows and shrinks as the climate changes. The ice sheets can be more than one mile (1.6 km) thick.

Great Depression—A time in American history beginning in 1929 and lasting for several years when many businesses failed and millions of people lost their jobs.

Hydroelectric—A way of generating electricity that uses water instead of burning oil or coal.

Lewis and Clark—Explorers Meriwether Lewis and William Clark led an expedition from 1804-1806. The expedition explored the unknown territory west of the Mississippi River.

World War I—A war that was fought mainly in Europe from 1914 to 1918, involving countries around the world. The United States entered the war in April 1917.

World War II—A conflict across the world, lasting from 1939-1945. The United States entered the war in December 1941.

Index